The Fruit of One Tree

Melanie Lotfali

When I get up I see our fruit bowl.

It is full of ripe yellow bananas.

Today I want to eat bananas
for breakfast, lunch, and dinner.

I peel a banana and take a big bite.

Then I see Maria selling mangos.

I remember how sweet
and slimy they are.

Maria sells me some mangos.

When I go to the tap to wash the mango juice from my chin, I see our paw paw tree.

Paw paw with lime juice.

My favourite!

Even with my belly full of paw paw, the orange tree catches my eye.

I pull an orange off the branch.

I peel it and break the orange ball into pieces.

I put them in my mouth one by one.

I start to think:

Bananas are yummy.
Mangos are sweet.
Paw paws are delicious.
Oranges are tasty.

What if we put them together?

What if we ate them mixed together?

That would be the best of all.

Yummy,
sweet,
delicious,
tasty
Fruit Salad!

O people of the world,
ye are all
the fruit of one tree and
the leaves of one branch.

~ Bahá'í Writings ~

Copyright © 2013 Melanie Lotfali

The Fruit of One Tree by Melanie Lotfali is licensed under a Creative Commons Attribution-NonCommercial-ShareAlike 4.0 International License.

ISBN 978-0-9945926-1-3

www.ingramcontent.com/pod-product-compliance
Lightning Source LLC
Chambersburg PA
CBHW042229010526
44113CB00046B/2949